ANIMAL SAFARI

Baboons

by Megan Borgert-Spaniol

BLASTOFF! READERS

BELLWETHER MEDIA · MINNEAPOLIS, MN

Note to Librarians, Teachers, and Parents:

Blastoff! Readers are carefully developed by literacy experts and combine standards-based content with developmentally appropriate text.

Level 1 provides the most support through repetition of high-frequency words, light text, predictable sentence patterns, and strong visual support.

Level 2 offers early readers a bit more challenge through varied simple sentences, increased text load, and less repetition of high-frequency words.

Level 3 advances early-fluent readers toward fluency through increased text and concept load, less reliance on visuals, longer sentences, and more literary language.

Level 4 builds reading stamina by providing more text per page, increased use of punctuation, greater variation in sentence patterns, and increasingly challenging vocabulary.

Level 5 encourages children to move from "learning to read" to "reading to learn" by providing even more text, varied writing styles, and less familiar topics.

Whichever book is right for your reader, Blastoff! Readers are the perfect books to build confidence and encourage a love of reading that will last a lifetime!

This edition first published in 2013 by Bellwether Media, Inc.

No part of this publication may be reproduced in whole or in part without written permission of the publisher. For information regarding permission, write to Bellwether Media, Inc., Attention: Permissions Department, 5357 Penn Avenue South, Minneapolis, MN 55419.

Library of Congress Cataloging-in-Publication Data
Borgert-Spaniol, Megan, 1989-
  Baboons / by Megan Borgert-Spaniol.
     p. cm. – (Blastoff! readers: animal safari)
  Includes bibliographical references and index.
  Summary: "Developed by literacy experts for students in kindergarten through grade three, this book introduces baboons to young readers through leveled text and related photos"–Provided by publisher.
  ISBN 978-1-60014-767-8 (hardcover : alk. paper)
  1. Baboons–Juvenile literature. I. Title.
QL737.P93B67 2013
599.8'65–dc23
                                        2011053015

Printed in the United States of America, North Mankato, MN.

Contents

What Are Baboons?

Baboons are large monkeys. They live on **savannahs** and rocky cliffs.

Baboons have brown or gray hair. Most males have a **mane** that covers their shoulders.

mane

Eating

Baboons eat grasses, seeds, and **insects**. Sometimes they hunt young antelopes and other small animals.

Their favorite meal is fruit. Baboons fill their cheeks with fruit so others cannot take it.

Troops

Baboons live in **troops**. They bark and make faces to **communicate**.

Baboons **groom** one another every day. One baboon picks insects and **ticks** off the other.

Females work together to care for the young. Mothers carry their babies on their backs.

Predators

Baboons show their teeth to scare away lions, hyenas, and other **predators**.

They climb trees
to escape danger.
They even sleep in
trees to stay safe.
Good night, baboon!

Glossary

communicate—to share messages or feelings with one another

groom—to clean

insects—small animals with six legs and hard outer bodies; insect bodies are divided into three parts.

mane—long, thick hair on the neck and shoulders of some animals

predators—animals that hunt other animals for food

savannahs—grasslands with very few trees

ticks—small animals with eight legs; ticks suck the blood of larger animals.

troops—groups of baboons that eat, sleep, and travel together

To Learn More

AT THE LIBRARY

Gosman, Gillian. *Baboons*. New York, N.Y.: PowerKids Press, 2012.

Horowitz, Dave. *Soon, Baboon, Soon*. New York, N.Y.: G.P. Putnam's Sons, 2005.

McCall Smith, Alexander. *Akimbo and the Baboons*. New York, N.Y.: Bloomsbury Children's Books, 2008.

ON THE WEB

Learning more about baboons is as easy as 1, 2, 3.

1. Go to www.factsurfer.com.

2. Enter "baboons" into the search box.

3. Click the "Surf" button and you will see a list of related Web sites.

With factsurfer.com, finding more information is just a click away.

Index